Once upon a Pancake

FOR YOUNG STORYTELLERS

Stories We
Write Together

PFANNKUCHEN PRESS

WRITTEN BY

THAT'S YOU!
WRITE YOUR NAMES

STARTED BY Rick Benger

LEAD ILLUSTRATION BY Maddie Egremont

EDITED BY Karin Fisher-Golton

COVER DESIGN BY Kristen Haff

HOW THIS BOOK WORKS

STEP ONE

Grab a pen, pick any story inside, and come up with what happens next. Write a little or a lot. Make it silly, scary, poetic, action-packed, magical. Go wherever your imagination takes you.

STEP TWO

Pass the pen. It's someone else's turn to write.

STEP THREE

Repeat! Keep taking turns. Giggle, make mistakes, help each other. When you finish, you'll have a unique story that only you and your friends could have created.

HAVE FUN!
RICK

Leon can hardly believe it. He's really here, in the stadium, for the World Cup semi-final, with five of his best friends from his soccer team. They've even made special shirts to spell out the name of their favorite player, Bobby Brooks.

They get a mountain of drinks and snacks, then find their seats. In all their excitement they forget to sit in the right order—of course they should be spelling B-R-O-O-K-S. Instead they're spelling K-R-O-B-O-S.

STORY #1

Big. Fat. Mistake.

...CONTINUED

WHAT DOES
KROBOS DO?

Nobody had seen Old Man Jenkins in twenty years, and Mo was determined to find out why.

Every night, Mo looked out from his bedroom window, with binoculars, across the lake at the house where Old Man Jenkins lived. The only sign that Old Man Jenkins was still alive was the mellow candlelight dancing on the curtains in an upstairs window. And sometimes, when it was an especially calm night, Mo heard a bone-tingling sound carry over the lake. It sounded like

....

....

....

....

....

STORY #2

STORY #2

"Can you keep a secret?" asked Julia.

I thought about it for a moment. The real answer was no. Secrets wriggle and bubble inside me until I burst and out they come.

"To be honest, probably not," I said, feeling pretty good about being honest.

"I'll tell you anyway," she said. "Last night I

STORY #3

DID THE SECRET
STAY SECRET?

Rosa had done nothing wrong.

Well, that's not exactly true. The instructions inside her new toy kit, the Robo-Master-Maker Special Edition, *did* say never to make anything during a thunderstorm. And Rosa had to admit that it was a little thundery and a tiny bit stormy when she completed her latest masterpiece, which she named

SOUNDS BAD.
WHAT DID ROSA'S
MASTERPIECE DO?

KEEP GOING...

STORY #4

...CONTINUED

WHOA. IS
THAT ROSA'S
MASTERPIECE
OR ANOTHER
ROBOT?

STORY #4

STORY #4

May 15th

Dear Diary,

I saw the future in my dreams again. That's 3 times now. They can't all be coincidences, can they? I'm freaking out!!

First, there was that dream where the floor in our classroom was lava and it was a gazillion degrees and everyone's books were on fire. And then the next day there was an actual fire in the school cafeteria, and we all got evacuated.

Then there was the dream about

And then the next day

And this morning I dreamed

Should I tell anyone? What if my dreams are making these things happen?

STORY #5

May 16th

Dear Diary,

It's my first time on an airplane. I'm in my seat, excited to finally know what takeoff feels like, looking out the window at the baggage workers who look like little Lego people on little Lego carts.

"Hi there," says somebody from the aisle seat. I turn around to say hello, but only manage a weird, gurgling "Hrrghh."

It's .... On my plane. Talking to me. For real.

SOUNDS LIKE SOMEONE FAMOUS. WHO?

STORY #6

It was official: Alana was a queen—the new queen of a place called Hippotopia, according to a boy with lilac-colored skin who appeared, bowed before her, and said, "Alana, my queen! At last I've found you. You must come with me. We don't have much time, because ....

....

....

....

....

....

....

....

....

....

....

To get to the school bus stop, Emi had to walk past the house with the vicious, beastly, terrifying hellhound.

At first, she dreaded walking alone. But over time she learned how to sneak by, quiet as the moon, light as the clouds. She didn't realize it yet, but she was becoming a ninja.

STORY #8

FINISH THE COMIC!

WHAT DID EMI USE HER NINJA SKILLS FOR?

STORY #8

We returned from winter break to find a statue of ....

....

in front of our school. No one knew how it got there,   *← ADD A NAME*

least of all me and my friend ....

But our principal, Mrs. Fong, called us into her office and said, "I know you

two are responsible. If you don't confess now, you'll be expelled."

    "We didn't do it!" we pleaded in chorus.

    "Lying will only make matters worse," said Mrs. Fong.   *UH-OH*

KEEP GOING...

DRAW THE
STATUE →

STORY #9

...CONTINUED

HOW DID THE
STATUE GET
THERE?

STORY #9

DID THEY PROVE
THEY WERE
INNOCENT?

Every seven years, at the first dawn of spring, a giant tree in Lotusville blooms with edible purple flowers that last for exactly one week.

They call it the .... tree because the flowers taste delicious—so delicious, in fact, that for the whole week all the grown-ups in Lotusville simply hang around the tree smiling, chatting, and munching away. They don't hustle or bustle. They don't frown or fret. Life is good, and worries can wait.

It's a story as old as Lotusville that any child who eats a special flower will turn into a ghost. But James is skeptical. He's never seen a ghost-child. "What if that's just a story told to stop us children from having fun?" he wonders. Maybe he should try a flower. Just one.

STORY #10

A t last, I have my own bedroom.

My parents told me I can I decorate it any way I like, with one condition:

....

WHAT'S THE CATCH?

DECORATE
THE ROOM

The whole country hasn't had hypernet for five days.

Everyone's losing it. Mom and Dad don't know what to do without their BusyBots. My sister is carrying on like she's the only one who has to suffer, boo-hoo, and all she's really missing out on is that stupid series about old English people.

I have a real reason for losing it—I need to figure out what a Zaggzok is. And who Professor Vincent is. Otherwise my friend Jason will rot in jail on Mars.

Okay, okay, you're thinking, who said anything about Mars? Cool your jetpack! I'm getting to that, like right now.

Jason's parents are mega-rich. They have their own rocket and go on vacation to this fancy resort on Mars every year. It's called .... Jason said maybe he can take me one day.

Anyway, this was the last message I got from Jason before the hypernet went down . . .

WHAT'S A
ZAGGZOK?

KEEP GOING...

STORY #12

...CONTINUED

"Are you Professor Vincent?" I whispered.

"Maybe. Who's asking?"

WHO IS
PROFESSOR
VINCENT?

STORY #12

IS JASON
RESCUED?

It was a normal Wednesday for Rayvan. School was okay, karate practice was awesome, and while walking home through the park she daydreamed about pizza. Karate always made her want pizza.

So she was walking, triple-pepperoni on her mind, when she saw a stick on the ground next to the giant willow tree and thought, "Huh, a magic wand." Then she thought, "Huh, I'm going crazy."

But wand or stick, it called to her. It looked like

STORY #13

Can I tell you something embarrassing?

I hated it when Grandma moved in with us. I know that's not nice. But I only hated it because it meant I had to share a room with my brother, Liam, and he's definitely not nice.

It's turning out great, though. Grandma is super fun. She is an awesome dancer, and she ....

....

Grandma is also a bit of a daredevil. She comes up with wild schemes and convinces me and Liam to play along. ....

.... SUCH AS?

....

....

....

....

....

....

....

....

....

....

....

STORY #14

Now of course Emory knew that throwing a disc in class would mean instant detention. But the disc in question was a brand new birthday gift from his friend Tyler. It would be rude not to seem excited. And Tyler was only like six feet away. And Mrs. O'Callaghan wasn't looking.

Emory's throw was perfect, sort of, almost. But Tyler

....

....

....

....

....

STORY #15

STORY #15

In the town of Little Creek, all music was gone.

When Aisha strummed her guitar, there was no thrum. When Simon struck his bass drum, it didn't go *bom*. And when Benjamin blew into his hands to play the national anthem in farts, the farts were silent.

No music, not a single note nor beat, was heard in all of Little Creek for weeks and weeks—until Aisha woke up in the night to the most enchanting, most beautiful guitar playing she'd ever heard. It was coming from outside. She put on a jacket, tiptoed past her parents' bedroom, and

WHO WAS PLAYING?

WHAT HAD HAPPENED
TO THE MUSIC?

STORY #16

FILL IN THE COMIC!

Rohan fell asleep, faceplanted on his desk, and dropped his pen on the floor. Again. Everyone laughed. Again.

It wasn't his fault that he kept falling asleep in class. He had to fight crime at night. And lately, there had been a whole lot of crime.

He bent down to pick up his pen and noticed something on the underside of his desk.

Meet me at locker E307 at lunch time. Come alone.

B.G.

WHO IS "B.G."?

KEEP GOING... STORY #17

A BIG BOX FOR A BIG FINISH!

"I dare you," she says.

I know, I know. I shouldn't feel like I have to do stuff just because someone dares me. But I can't help it. Especially because it's Gabriela who's doing the daring.

WHAT'S THE DARE?

GABRIELA

STORY #18

Dante thought that Mr. Van der Snoot's History of Mystery class was boring—memorizing silly words and old symbols, and studying ugly plants and magic spells that hadn't worked for centuries, ever since the Great Disempowerment.

But now he really, really wished he had paid more attention in class.

.... WHY? WHAT
.... HAPPENED?

....

....

....

....

....

....

....

....

....

Dante tried to remember the right spell.

" .... !" he cried.

....

.... WHAT SPELL DID
                                                                           DANTE USE?
.... DID IT WORK?

....

STORY #19

WHO ARE
THEY?

KEEP GOING . . .

STORY #19

...CONTINUED

....

....

....

....

....

....

....

....

....

....

....

....

....

....

....

WHAT'S IN THE
BOTTLES?

STORY #19

STORY #19

Emma has always been a scientist.

Her first word was *why*. Ever since, it's been her favorite word—along with *what, how, where, who,* and *when*. All the best words were questions too.

"What," she asked herself one day, "does sand look like up close?" So she got out her microscope and looked . . . and she was gobsmacked! It looked like

....

....

....

Emma decided to look at other ordinary things up close. She looked at ....

....

....

....

....

....

WHAT IS THIS? HINT: SOMEONE WHO STUDIES OR COLLECTS THEM IS CALLED A LEPIDOPTERIST

....

Next, she decided to look at ....

And then something crazy

happened ....

....

....

....

WHAT DID SHE
SEE? DRAW IT!

....

....

....

....

....

....

....

....

....

....

STORY #20

WANT MORE STORIES?

AT **ONCEUPONAPANCAKE.COM** YOU'LL FIND:

the full children's series

free teacher's guides and story packs

the coffee table book (for grown-ups)

Published in the United States in 2019 by Pfannkuchen Press LLC, California.

Copyright © 2019 by Rick Benger. All rights reserved.

Original illustrations by Matej Beg in story 1; by Maddie Egremont in stories 7, 9, 11, and 17; by Satria Wahyu in story 8; and by Onofrio Orlando in story 15. All original illustrations are owned by Pfannkuchen Press. All other images and adapted images are licensed via Shutterstock.

The Library of Congress Cataloging-in-Publication data have been applied for.

ISBN: 978-0-9993961-3-1

First edition. Printed and bound in Canada.